Mel Bay Presents

Introduction to
Playing Flute

by Joe Maroni

1 2 3 4 5 6 7 8 9 0

Visit us on the Web at www.melbay.com — E-mail us at email@melbay.com

INTRODUCTION TO FLUTE PLAYING

By Joe Maroni

The Ideal Method Book for Beginning Flute Players

This method book progresses in a step-by-step fashion. Every lesson builds on those that came before, giving students a chance to practice what they have learned and reinforcing skills that will be used over and over.

The primary emphasis is to develop the four essential concepts for learning to play the flute:

> ➤ Learning the names of the notes on the music staff
> ➤ Learning the value of the notes and how to count them
> ➤ Learning how to finger the notes on the flute
> ➤ Learning to play high and low sounds

As new notes are introduced on the lines and spaces of the music staff, the note name, note value, method of counting, and fingering of the note on the flute is clearly illustrated.

Each of the essential music elements is presented clearly and sequentially. Each presentation is followed by several exercises and original melodies that are specifically designed to develop reading ability, technique, and musicianship. Students will understand and develop each newly learned music concept as they progress from lesson to lesson.

The unique feature of this flute method book is that the lessons progress in a logical manner conducive to learning to play the flute. Concessions are not made to accommodate playing with other instruments which is typical in band series methods. However, after mastering the first three lessons, the student will be able to begin playing the material in any band series book.

TABLE OF CONTENTS

PARTS OF THE FLUTE

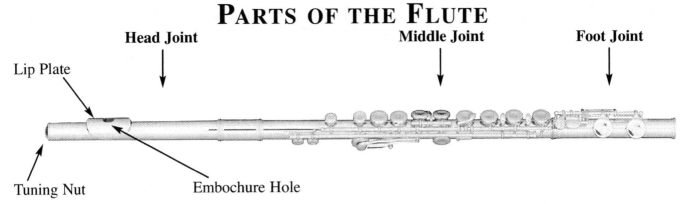

Lip Plate · **Head Joint** · **Middle Joint** · **Foot Joint** · **Tuning Nut** · **Embochure Hole**

PUTTING THE FLUTE TOGETHER

- Twist the foot joint onto the end of the middle joint and line up the foot joint keys with the middle joint keys.
- Twist the head joint onto the other end of the middle joint and line up the embouchure hole with the middle joint keys.

PRODUCING A SOUND WITH THE HEAD JOINT

- Place the head joint against your lower lip with the embouchure hole in the center of your lip.
- Keep the head joint straight making sure it does not tilt. Keep your head up and look straight ahead.
- Put your lips together. Slightly tighten the corners of your mouth leaving just enough space between the center of your lips to allow air to pass through.
- The tongue is needed for making a clear and precise beginning to a note. Place the tip of your tongue at the top of your teeth; using the syllable "T", blow air across the embouchure hole to produce a tone. Fast air produces a high tone; slower air produces a low tone.

HOLDING THE FLUTE

- Hold the flute straight making sure it does not tilt at an angle.
- Let the flute rest on the thumb of your right hand.
- Curve your fingers over the flute keys.
- Press the keys with the tips of your fingers.

TUNING THE FLUTE

- The pitch of your flute can be adjusted by moving the head joint in or out of the middle joint.
- Pull the head joint out to lower the pitch. Push the head joint in to raise the pitch.

ADJUSTING THE TUNING NUT

- On the end of the cleaning rod there is a notch that is used to center the tuning nut inside the head joint.
- Slide the tuning rod into the head joint.
- Loosen the head joint cap and slide the tuning nut until the notch is centered in the embouchure hole.

CLEANING YOUR FLUTE

- Swab out the inside of your flute after each use.
- Clean your fingerprints off the outside of your flute after each use.
- Rinse out the head joint with warm soapy water at least once a week and dry it with a lint free cloth.
- Always store your flute in the case; never leave it out to accumulate dust.
- Be extra careful not to drop or bump your flute.

FLUTE MAINTENANCE KIT

- Flute cleaning rod
- Lint-free cloth for swabbing the inside of your flute
- Silver polishing cloth for cleaning the outside of your flute
- Cleaning paper for removing moisture, oil, and dust from the pads

PRACTICE TIPS

- Set aside a certain time each day to practice in a quiet room where it is easy to concentrate on what you are practicing without being disturbed.
- Listen! Everything else in practicing depends on you listening to yourself.
- Listen to good flute players (invest in quality CDs and attend quality concerts).
- Take lessons! Get someone who can help you start correctly. Bad habits will limit your success, and they are hard to break!
- Use a music stand to ensure that you are playing with proper posture. The music stand should be adjusted so that you don't have to tilt your head or twist your body.
- Review previous lessons.

PRELIMINARIES

The Music Staff

The MUSIC STAFF consists of five LINES and four SPACES.

The Treble Clef Sign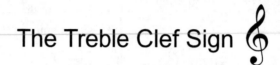

All music for flute has the TREBLE CLEF SIGN at the beginning of the staff.

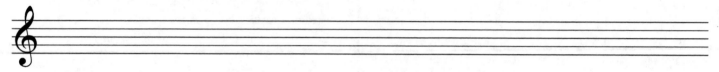

On a staff the notes are either on a line or in a space. The LINES and SPACES have letter names.

Line and Space Names

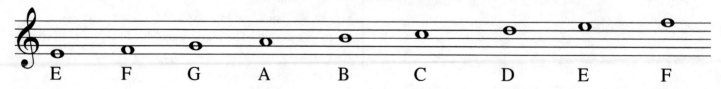

4

PRELIMINARIES
Measures and Barlines

BARLINES divide the STAFF into MEASURES.

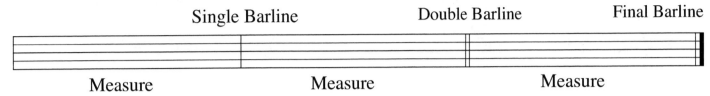

Single Barline   Double Barline   Final Barline

Measure   Measure   Measure

A Single Barline marks the end of a measure.

A Double Barline marks the end of a section of music.

A Final Barline marks the end of a music composition.

NOTES

Notes represent musical sounds.

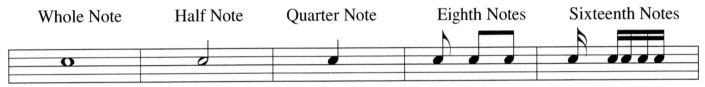

Whole Note   Half Note   Quarter Note   Eighth Notes   Sixteenth Notes

Eighth Notes are often grouped in twos. Sixteenth Notes are often grouped in fours.

RESTS

Rests represent silence.

Whole Rest   Half Rest   Quarter Rest   Eighth Rest   Sixteenth Rest

Time Signatures

At the beginning of every piece is a time signature which consists of two numbers; one on top of the other.

The top number indicates the number of beats in each measure.

The bottom number indicates the type of note that receives one beat; 4 = Quarter Note.

Count and tap your foot on every beat.

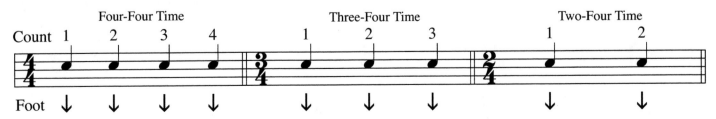

WHOLE NOTES AND WHOLE RESTS

Count and tap your foot.

Count and tap your foot.

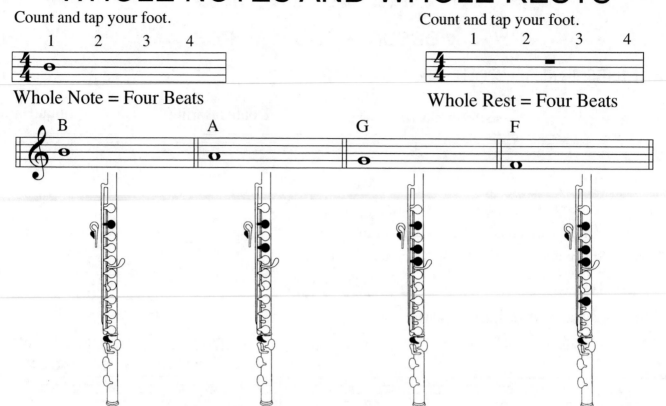

Whole Note = Four Beats

Whole Rest = Four Beats

In Four-Four Time there are four beats in each measure. Whole Notes and Whole Rests receive four beats. Tongue each note. Tap your foot on every beat.

HALF NOTES AND HALF RESTS

Count and tap your foot.

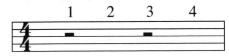

Half Rest = Two Beats

...ur beats in each measure. Half Notes and Half Rests receive two beats.
...t on every beat.

QUARTER NOTES AND QUARTER RESTS

Count and tap your foot.

Count and tap your foot.

Quarter Note = One Beat

Quarter Rest = One Beat

In Four-Four Time there are four beats in each measure. Quarter Notes and Quarter Rests receive one beat.

Tongue each note. Tap your foot on every beat.

MELODY STUDIES

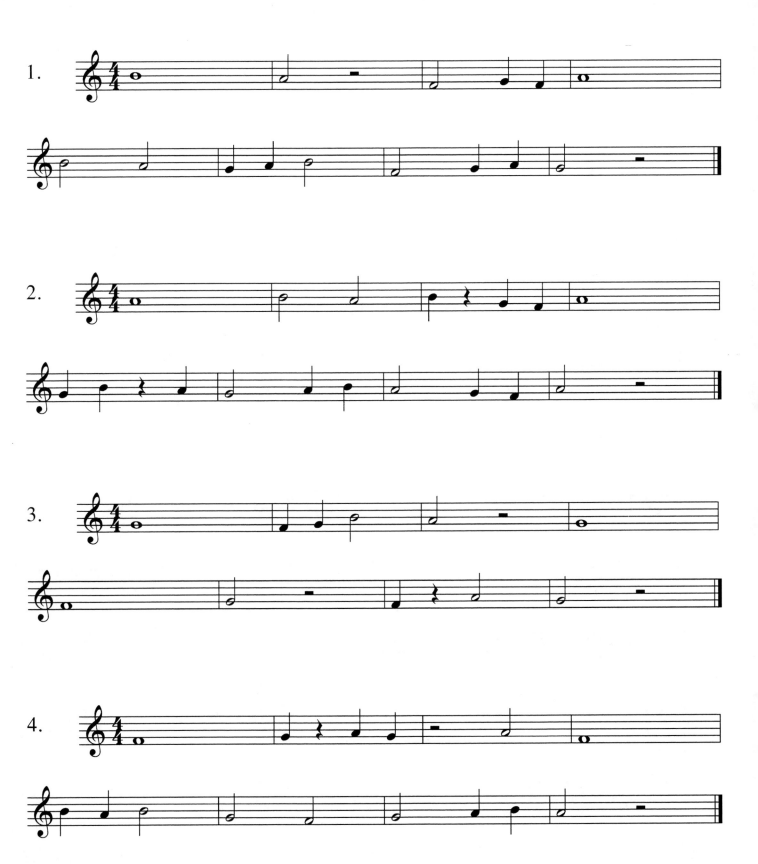

NEW NOTES

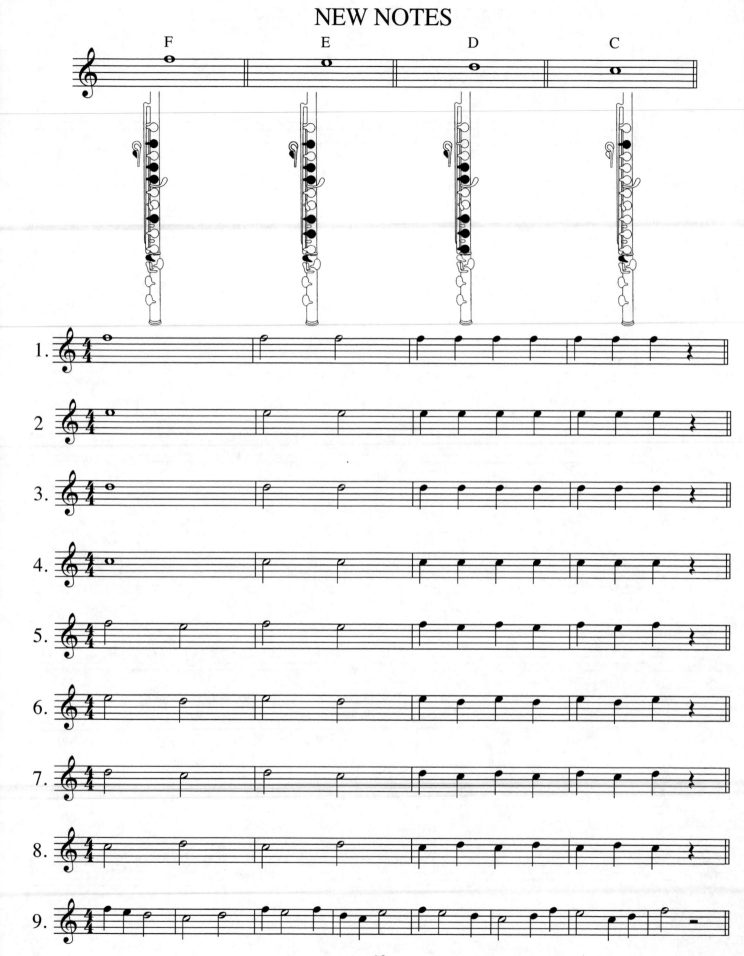

MELODY STUDIES

MELODY

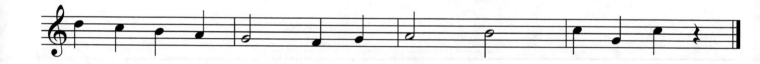

MELODY

HIGH NOTES ON LEDGER LINES

Ledger lines are short lines added above the staff for notes that are too high to be placed on the staff.

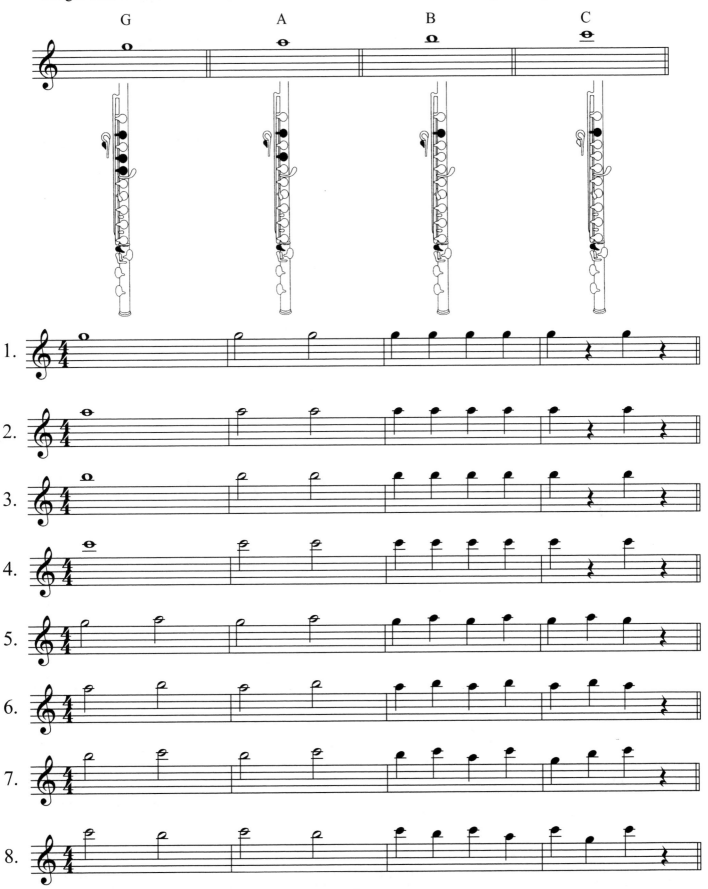

MELODY STUDIES

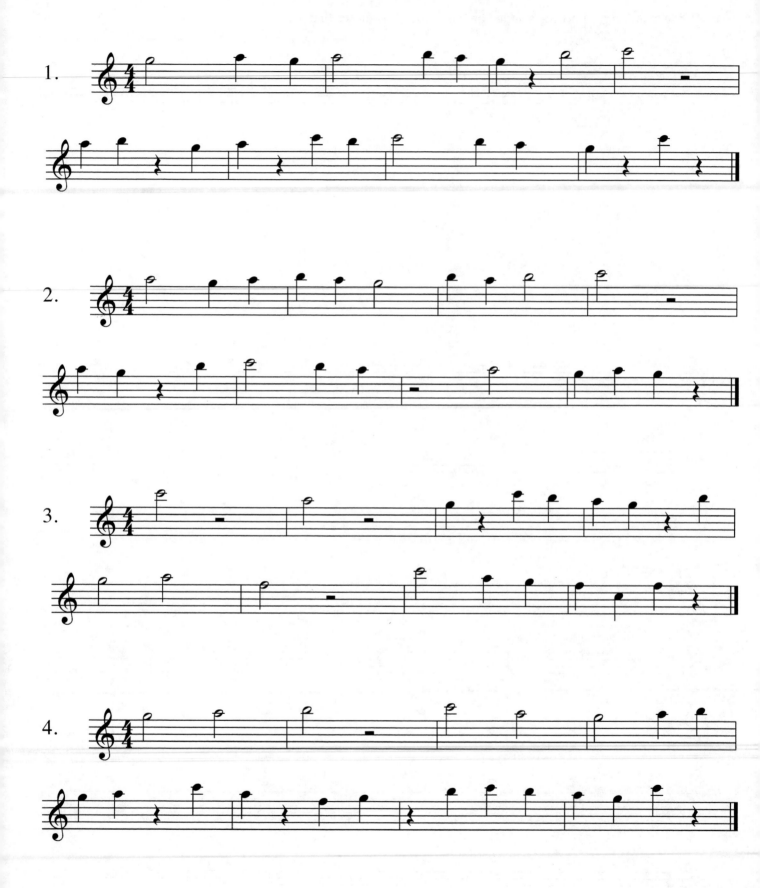

C MAJOR SCALE

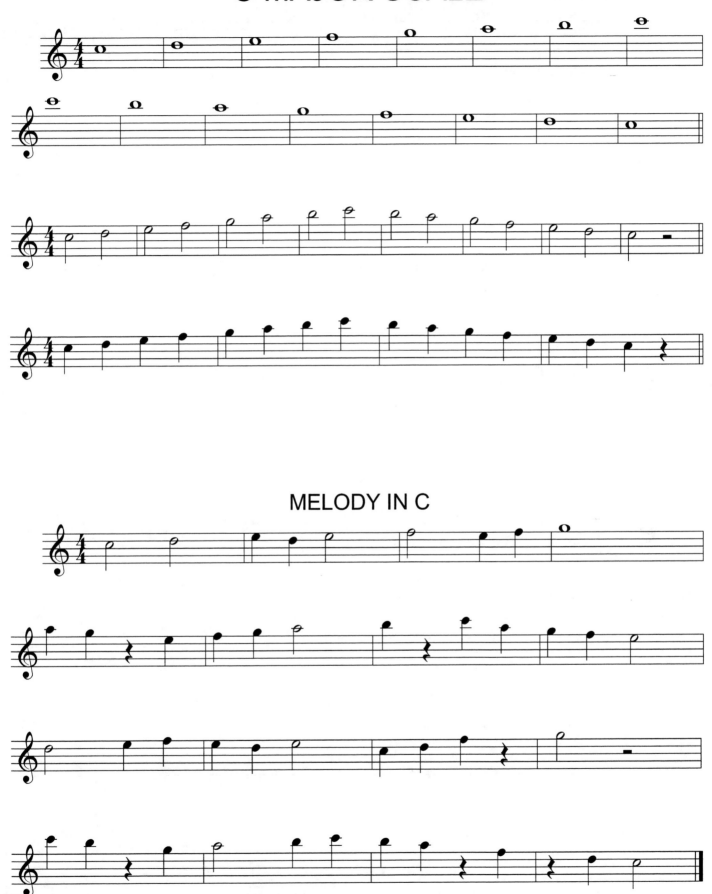

MELODY IN C

MELODY IN C

Andante (Slow)

mf (Medium Loud)

MELODY IN C

Andante

mf

16

THREE-FOUR TIME AND DOTTED HALF NOTES

In Three-Four Time there are three beats in each measure. The Quarter Note receives one beat.

A dot placed after a note increases the value of the note by ½.

A Half Note (♩) = 2 beats, the Dot (.) = ½ of a Half Note or one beat so the Dotted Half Note (♩.) = 3 beats.

C SCALE IN THREE-FOUR TIME

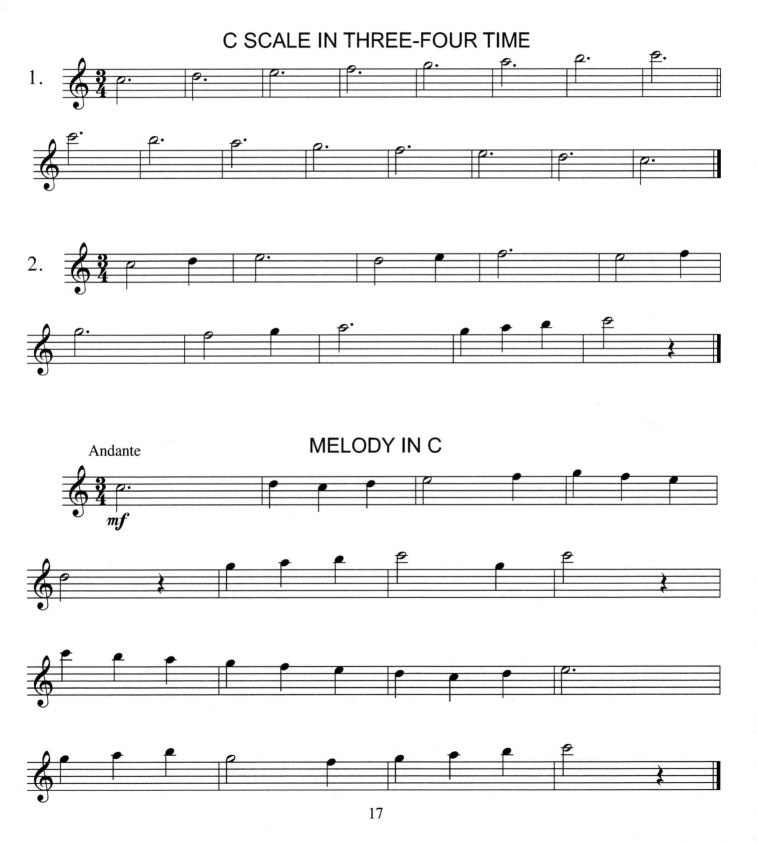

MELODY IN C

Andante

mf

ACCIDENTALS

Accidentals such as flats (♭) are used to temporarily change the pitch of a note.

A flat is used to lower the pitch of a note - such as B to B♭.

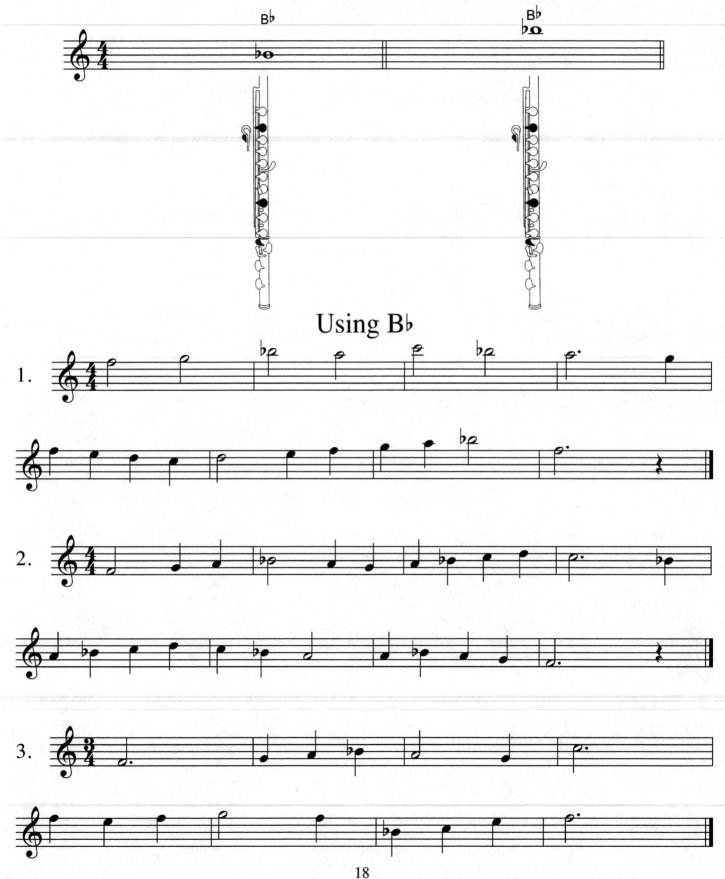

Using B♭

F MAJOR SCALE

A key signature at the beginning of each piece indicates the sharps or flats to be played in that piece.

The F Major Scale has one Flat which is B♭. Every time you see B, play it as B♭.

* Use B♭ in the key of F.

MELODY IN F

Use B♭ in the key of F.

Use B♭ in the key of F.

MELODY IN F

Moderato (Medium Fast)

mp (Medium Soft)

Use B♭ in the key of F.

MELODY IN F

Moderato

mp

20

Before you begin to play any piece, look at the key signature and the time signature.

MELODY IN F

MORE ACCIDENTALS

Accidentals such as sharps (♯) are used to temporarily change the pitch of a note.

A sharp (♯) is used to raise the pitch of a note - such as F to F♯.

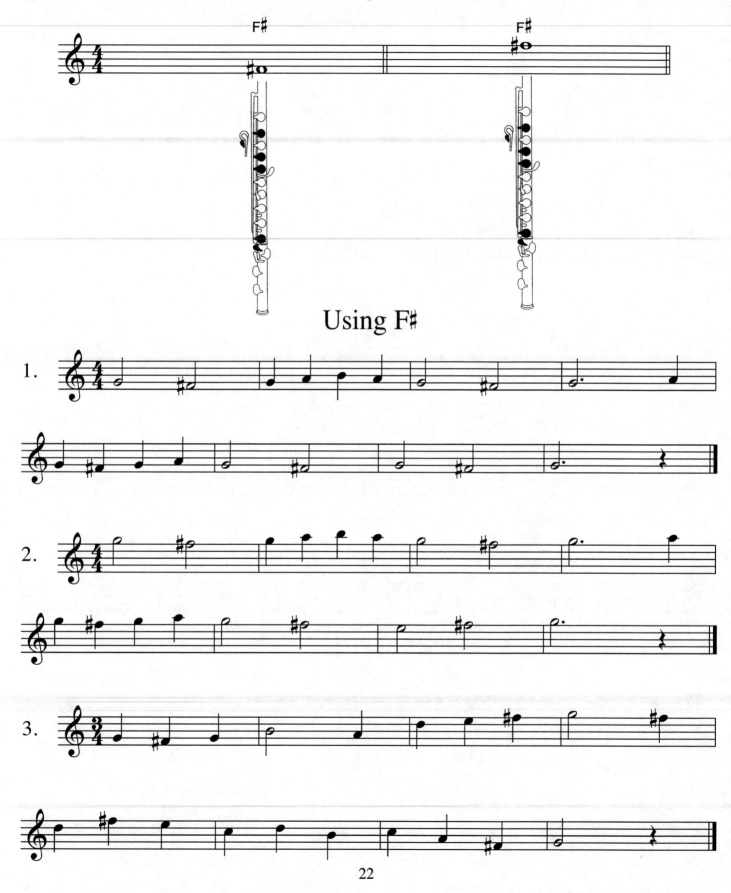

Using F♯

G MAJOR SCALE

A key signature at the beginning of each piece indicates the sharps or flats to be played in that piece.

The G Major Scale has one sharp which is F♯. Every time you see F, play it as F♯.

* Use F♯ in the key of G.

Use F♯ in the key of G.

MELODY IN G

FINGER EXERCISES IN G

Use F♯ in the key of G.

Two dots before a final barline indicate to repeat from the beginning.

Repeat each fingering exercise several times playing a little faster each time.

Use F♯ in the key of G.

MELODY IN G

COMMON TIME

Common Time is exactly the same as Four-Four Time. The **C** Symbol is used instead of the $\frac{4}{4}$ symbol.

Use F♯ in the key of G.

MELODY IN G

EIGHTH NOTES

An Eighth Note (♪) receives ½ of a beat.

Play two eighth notes in one beat.
The "+" means "and".

EIGHTH NOTE STUDIES

EIGHTH NOTE FINGERING STUDIES

Repeat each fingering exercise several times playing a little faster each time.

MELODY IN F

MELODY IN G

29

TWO-FOUR TIME

In Two-Four Time there are two beats in each measure.
The Quarter Note receives one beat.

MELODY IN C

(Repeat previous two measures)

(Repeat previous measure)

TIES

A **tie** connects two consecutive notes of the same pitch.

Do not tongue the second note. Play both notes as one continuous sound.

TIE EXERCISES

TIE STUDIES

MORE ACCIDENTALS

Accidentals such as **flats** (♭) are used to temporarily change the pitch of a note

A flat (♭) is used to lower the pitch of a note - such as E to E♭.

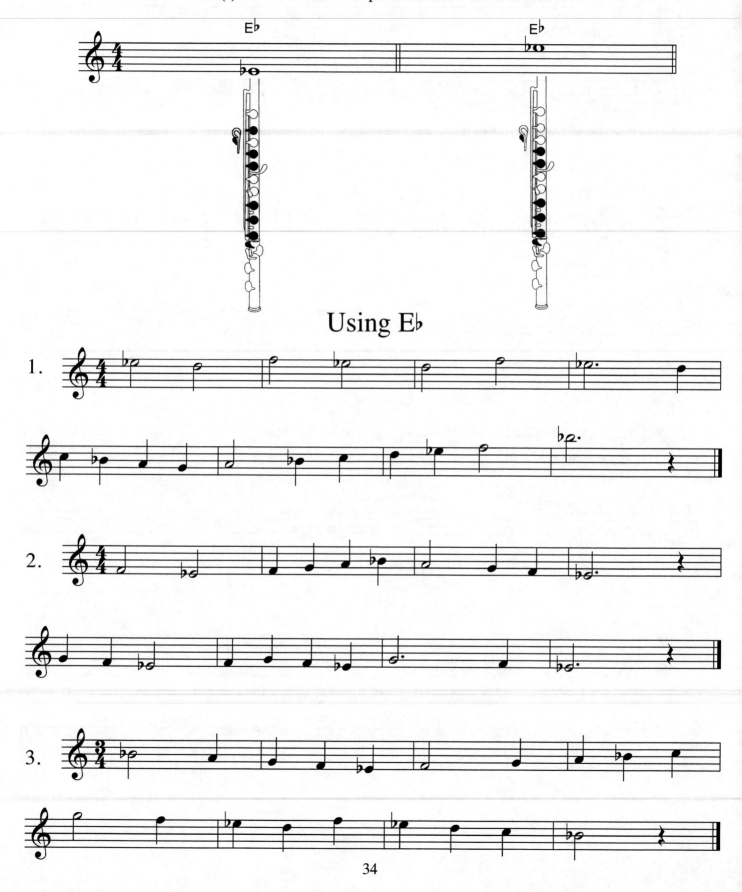

Using E♭

B♭ MAJOR SCALE

A key signature at the beginning of each piece indicates the sharps or flats to be played in that piece.

The B♭ Major Scale has two flats which are B♭ and E♭.

MELODY IN B♭

Use B♭ and E♭ in the key of B♭.

MELODY IN B♭

Use B♭ and E♭ in the key of B♭.

MELODY IN B♭

Slurs

A **slur** is a curved line placed above or below two or more notes of different pitches to indicate to play the notes smoothly, in one breath, without tonguing each note.

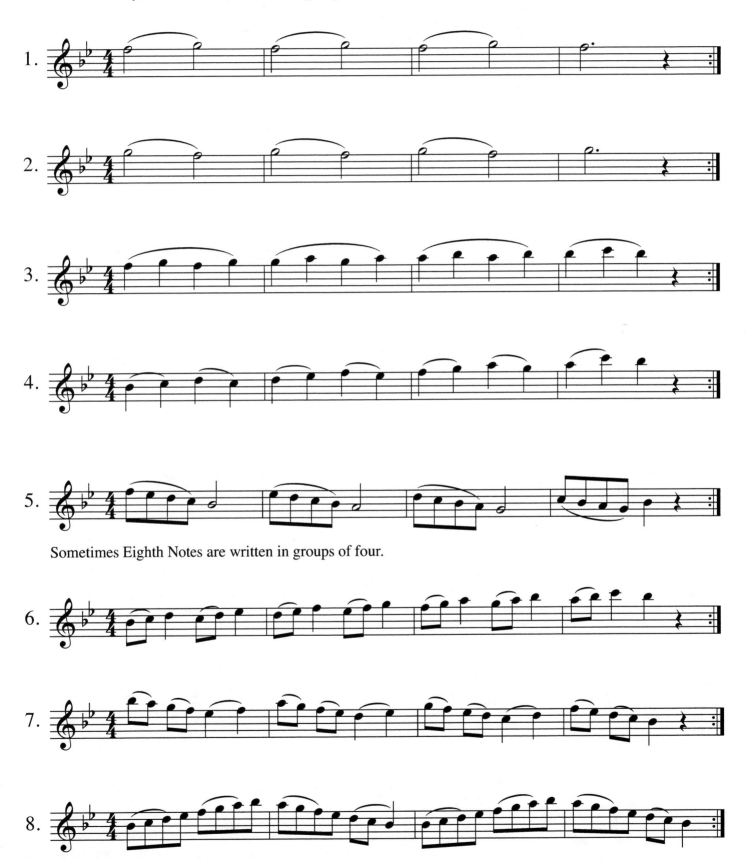

Sometimes Eighth Notes are written in groups of four.

Before you begin to play any piece, look at the key signature and the time signature.

MELODY IN B♭

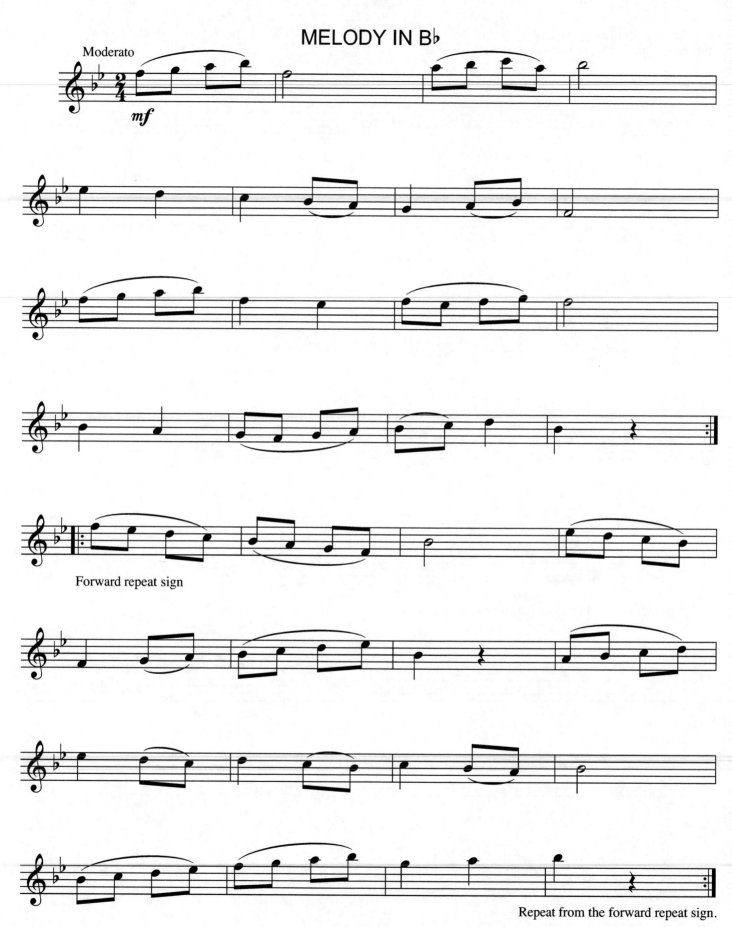

Forward repeat sign

Repeat from the forward repeat sign.

DOTTED QUARTER NOTES

A dot placed after a note increases the value of the note by ½.

A Quarter Note (♩) = 1 beat, the Dot (.) = ½ of a Quarter Note or ½ of a beat so the Dotted Quarter Note (♩.) = 1½ beats.

DOTTED QUARTER NOTE STUDIES

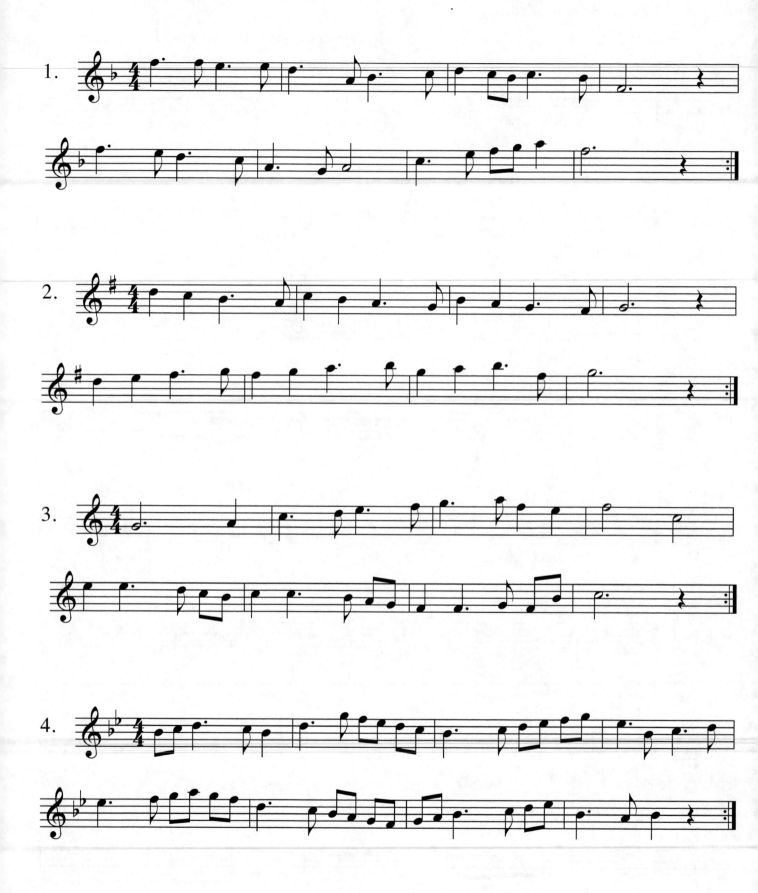

1st AND 2nd ENDINGS

Play through the first ending; repeat from the beginning, then skip the first ending and play the second ending.

MELODY IN B♭

NEW NOTES

Low E — Low D

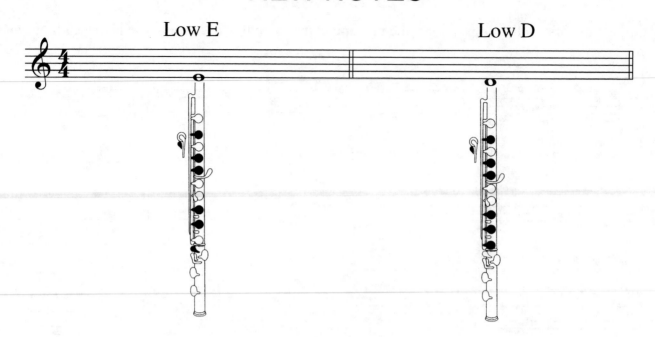

Using Low E and Low D

MORE ACCIDENTALS

Accidentals such as sharps (♯) are used to temporarily change the pitch of a note.

A sharp (♯) is used to raise the pitch of a note - such as C to C♯.

Slow air for low notes.   Fast air for high notes.

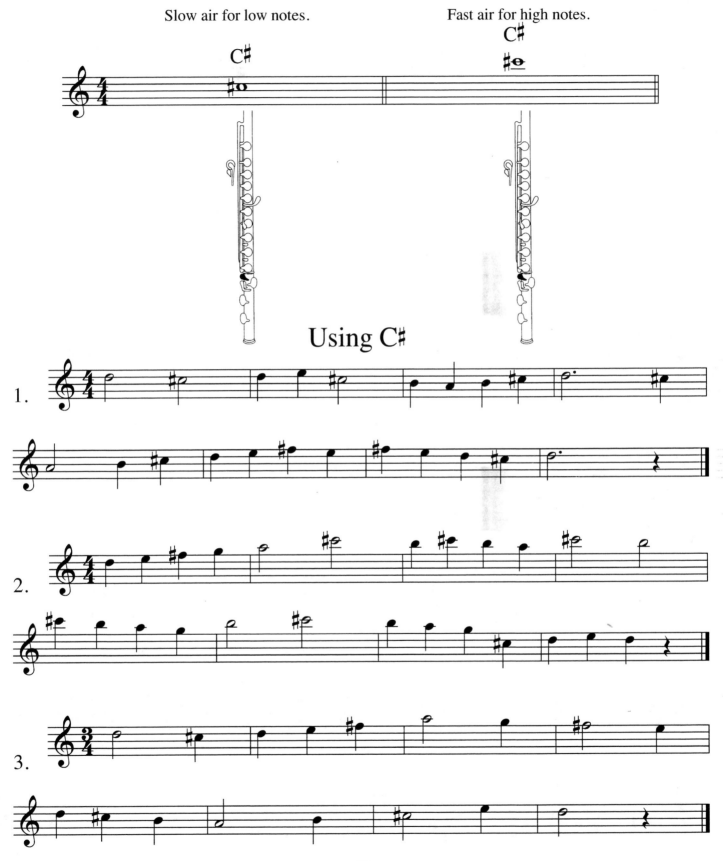

Using C♯

D MAJOR SCALE

A key signature at the beginning of each piece indicates the sharps or flats to be played in that piece.

The D Major Scale has two sharps which are F♯ and C♯.

* Use F♯ and C♯ in the key of D.

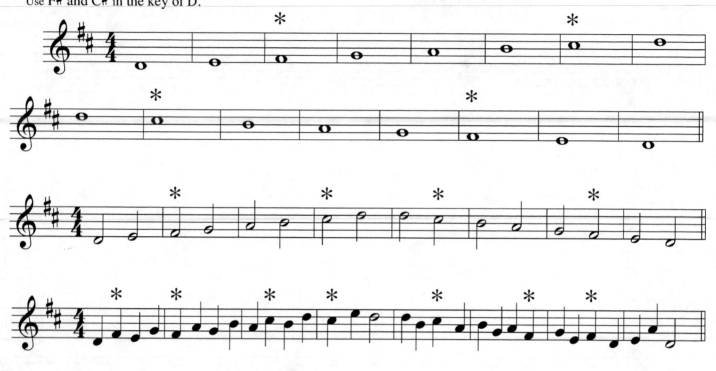

MELODY IN D

Use F♯ and C♯ in the key of D.

Use F# and C# in the key of D.

MELODY IN D

Use F# and C# in the key of D.

MELODY IN D

Before you begin to play any piece, look at the key signature and the time signature.

MELODY IN D

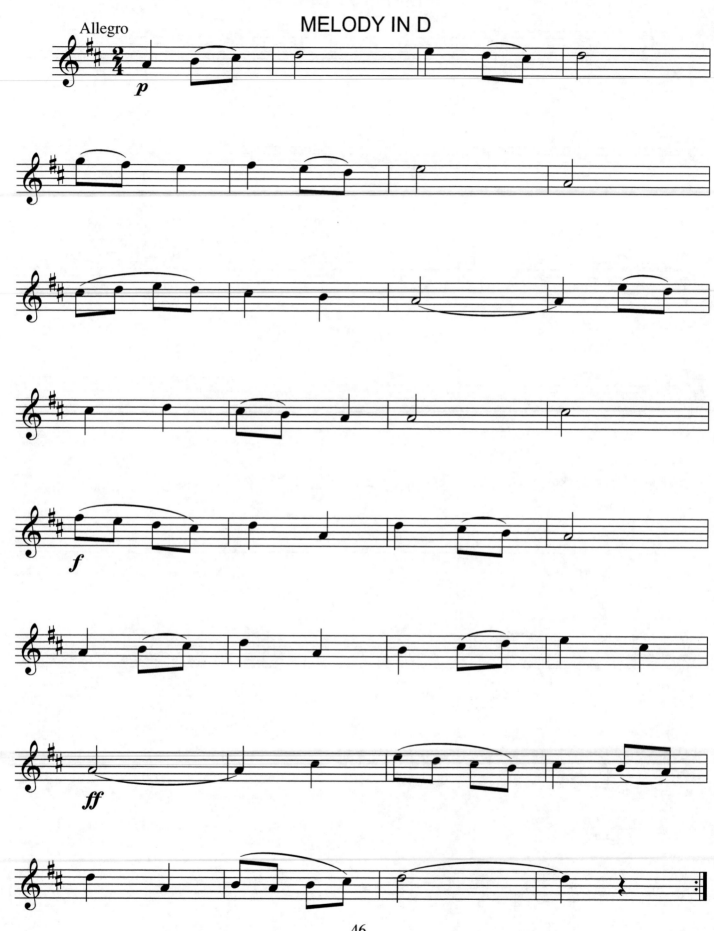

SIXTEENTH NOTES

A Sixteenth Note (♪) receives ¼ of a beat. Play four sixteenth notes in one beat.

SIXTEENTH NOTE STUDIES

MELODY IN C

Moderato

MELODY IN G

Moderato

COMBINING EIGHTH NOTES WITH SIXTEENTH NOTES

MELODY IN B♭

COMBINING EIGHTH NOTES WITH SIXTEENTH NOTES

MELODY IN F

MORE ACCIDENTALS

Accidentals such as flats (♭) are used to temporarily change the pitch of a note.

A flat (♭) is used to lower the pitch of a note - such as A to A♭.

Slow air for low notes.   Fast air for high notes.

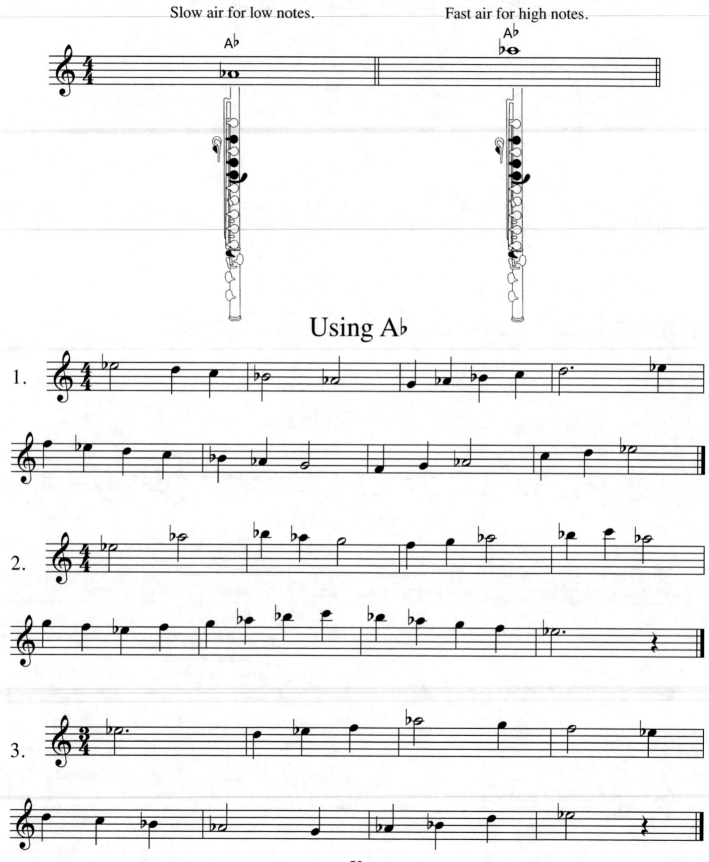

Using A♭

52

E♭ MAJOR SCALE

A key signature at the beginning of each piece indicates the sharps or flats to be played in that piece.

The E♭ Major Scale has three flats which are B♭, E♭, and A♭.

* Use B♭, E♭, and A♭ in the key of E♭.

Use B♭, E♭, and A♭ in the key of E♭.

MELODY IN E♭

Use B♭, E♭, and A♭ in the key of E♭.

MELODY IN E♭

Use B♭, E♭, and A♭ in the key of E♭.

MELODY IN E♭

MELODY IN E♭

Use B♭, E♭, and A♭ in the key of E♭.

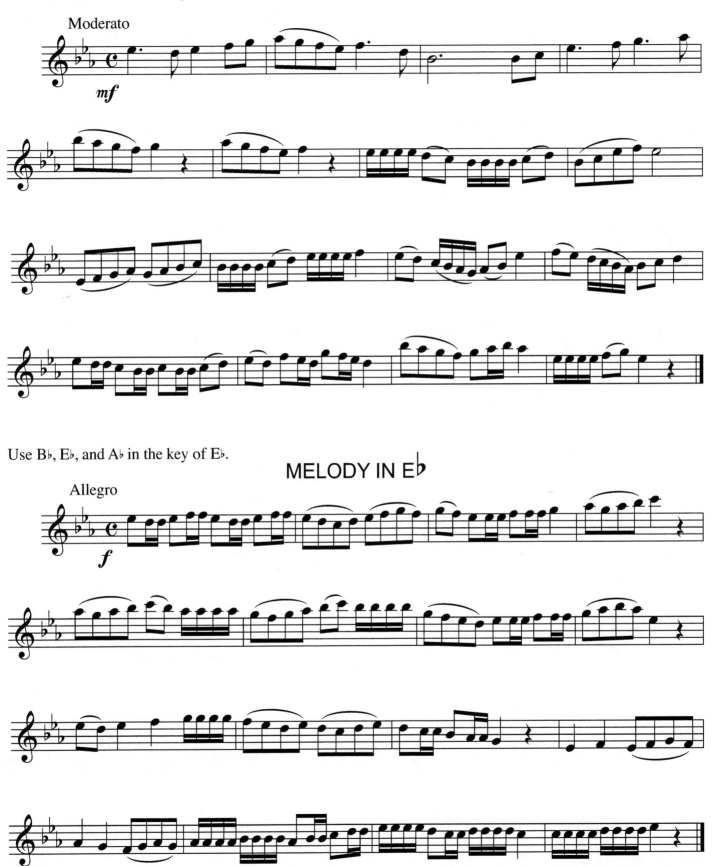

Use B♭, E♭, and A♭ in the key of E♭.

MELODY IN E♭

55

CUT TIME

Cut Time is Four-Four Time cut in half, hence Two-Two Time.

The note values in Cut Time are ½ that of Four-Four Time. In Cut Time there are two beats in each measure. Half Notes receive one beat. Whole Notes receive two beats. The ¢ symbol is used for Cut Time.

CUT TIME EXERCISES

The note values in Cut Time are ½ that of Four-Four Time. In Cut Time there are two beats in each measure. Half Notes receive one beat. Whole Notes receive two beats.

CUT TIME EXERCISES IN D

E♭ MELODY IN CUT TIME

MORE ACCIDENTALS

Accidentals such as sharps (♯) are used to temporarily change the pitch of a note.

A sharp (♯) is used to raise the pitch of a note - such as G to G♯.

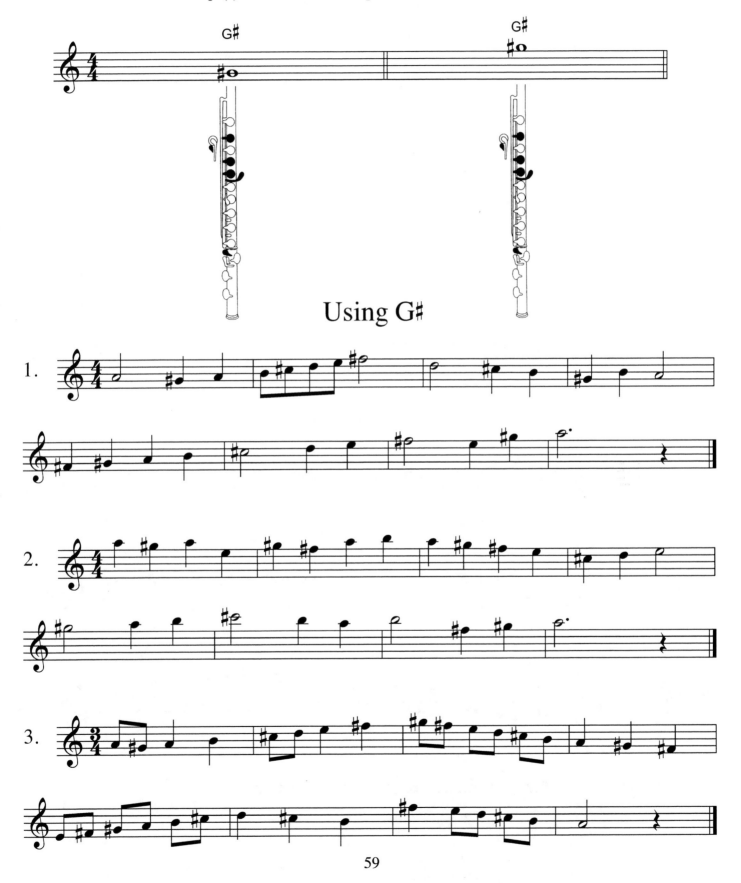

Using G♯

A MAJOR SCALE

A key signature at the beginning of each piece indicates the sharps or flats to be played in that piece.

The A major scale has three sharps which are F♯, C♯, and G♯.

* Use F♯, C♯, and G♯ in the key of A.

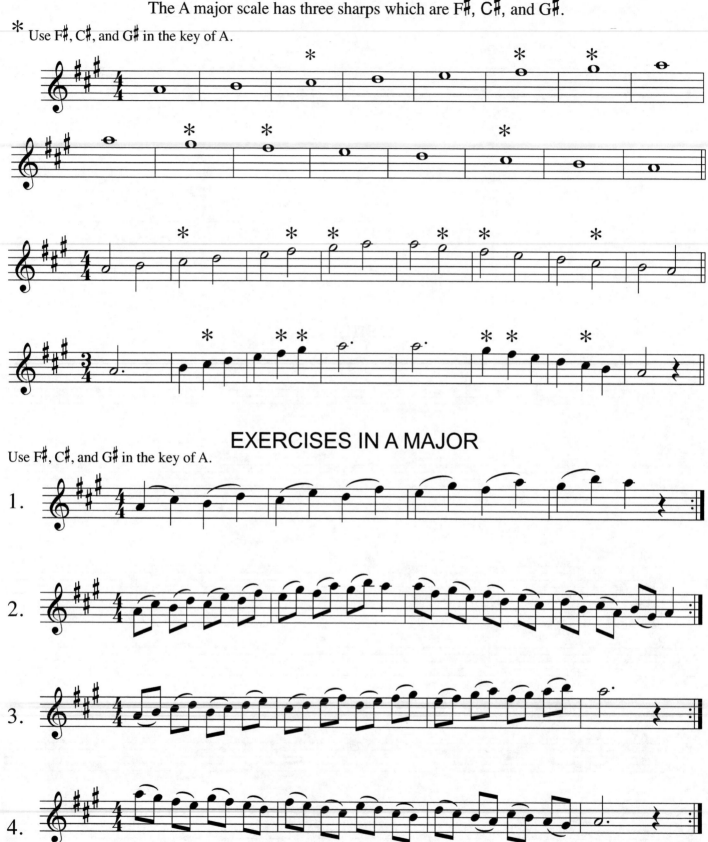

EXERCISES IN A MAJOR

Use F♯, C♯, and G♯ in the key of A.

SIX-EIGHT TIME

In Six-Eight Time there are six beats in each measure.

Eighth Notes (♪) and Eighth Rests (♪) receive one beat.

In Six-Eight time note values are double that of Four-Four time.

SIX-EIGHT TIME STUDIES

SIX-EIGHT MELODY IN D

SIX-EIGHT MELODY IN E♭

SIX-EIGHT MELODY IN F

SIX-EIGHT MELODY IN G

HIGH D, E, and F

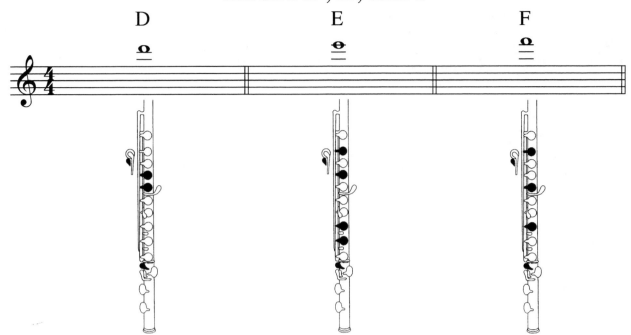

USING HIGH D, E, and F

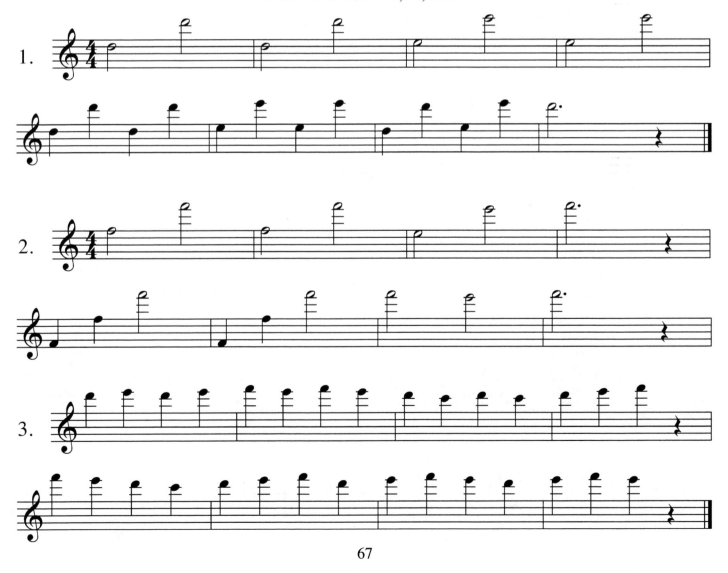

HIGH NOTE MELODY IN C

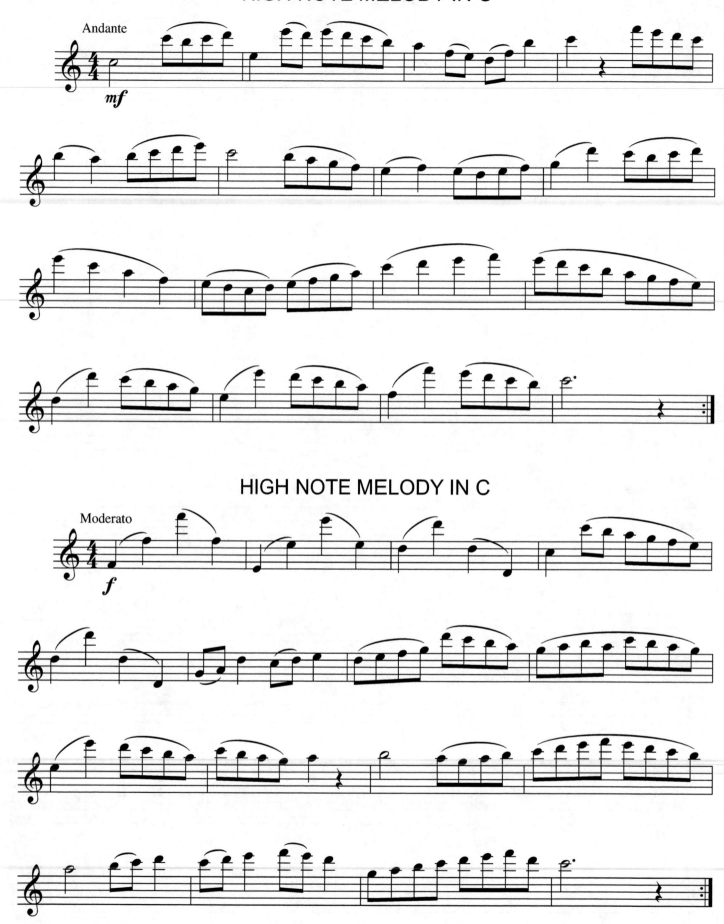

HIGH NOTE MELODY IN C

HIGH NOTE MELODY IN F

ENHARMONICS

Enharmonics are notes that sound the same and are fingered the same but are written differently - such as C# and Db.

A sharp # is used to raise the pitch of a note - such as F to F#.

A flat ♭ is used to lower the pitch of a note - such as B to B♭.

A natural ♮ is used to cancel a sharp or flat.

When a note is sharp or flat in a measure, the note should remain sharp or flat throughout the measure.

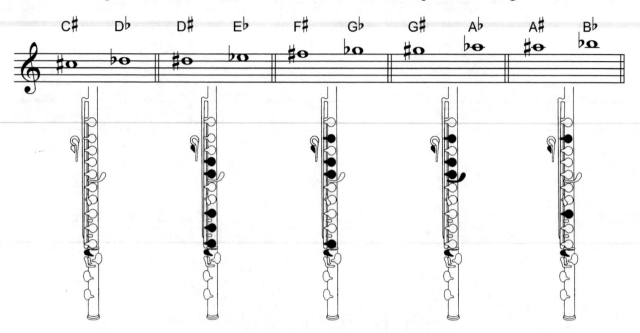

CHROMATIC SCALE

In general, use sharps (#) when going up the scale, use flats (♭)when going down the scale.

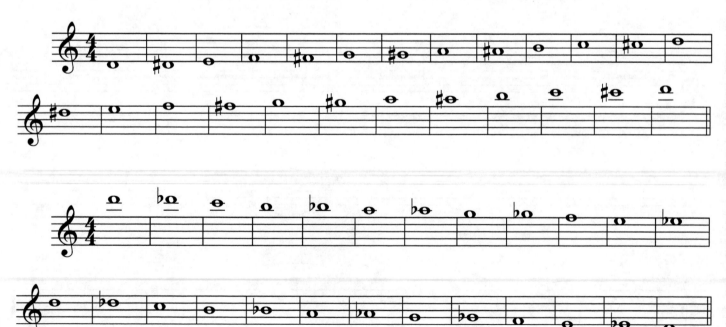

70

CHROMATIC MELODY

CHROMATIC MELODY

FLUTE FINGERING CHART

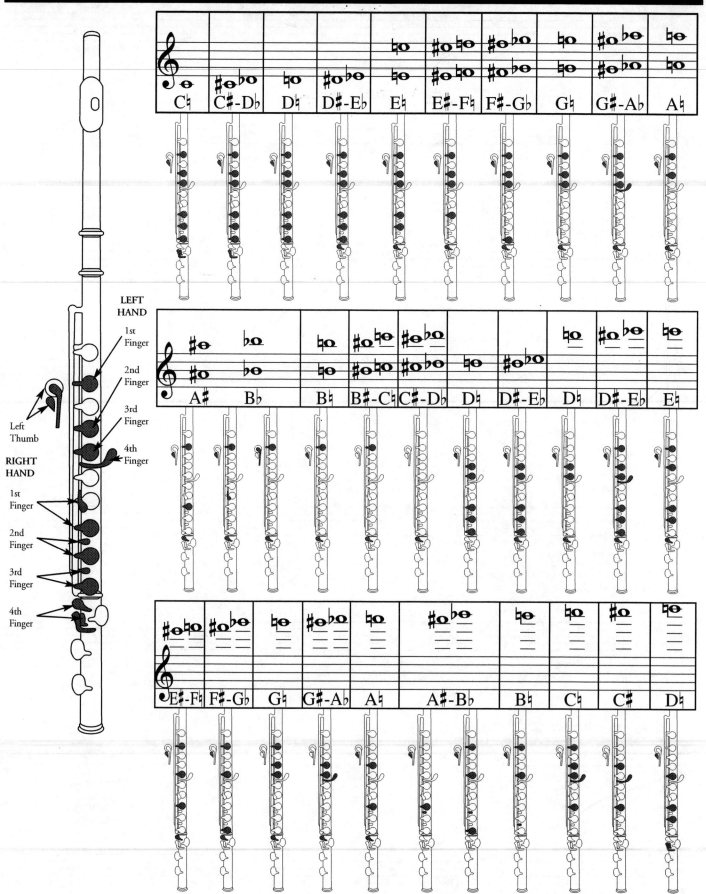

72